A Black Rose
and Other Poems

A Black Rose
and Other Poems

Shiva Rahel Swaminathan Strickland

Pineapple Poetry & Prose
Berkeley, California 2018

Copyright © 2018 by Shiva Rahel Swaminathan Strickland

All rights reserved. This book or any portion thereof may not be reproduced or used in any manner whatsoever without the express written permission of the publisher except for the use of brief quotations in a book review or scholarly journal.

First Printing, June 2018

ISBN 978-1-7324173-0-4

Pineapple Poetry & Prose
Berkeley, California

To my family, teachers, and friends.

Contents

The Sun Shines Bright 1
Polka-Dot the Great 2
Orange, Purple, and Pink 4
Many Mornings I Have Stood Here 5
A Black Rose 7
Possibilities 9
Illuminated 10
Ice Cream 11
Icicle 12
Seagull 13
Goodbye 14
The Zraveler Beep 15
Ode to Kiwis 17
Early Forest Morning 18
Lost in a Dream 19
Nothing Resists 20
My Freedeom 21
Pushed Around 22
So Credulous 23
My Bed 24
A Raindrop Has No Choice 25
California Lilacs 26

The Sun Shines Bright

The sun shines bright
over the gloomy night.
It warms up Spring
with its warm light
and washes away
all night frights.
It brings glowing happiness
to all the people that care:
there, there, and
everywhere.

Polka-Dot the Great

O, hail the one who bounces
up and down!
The one who reaches for
the rain!
O, great Polka-dot, what
do you see?

I see the people in need.
I see the ones who
are hard at work.
I see the ocean's crashing waves,
asking for something.
I tower over the land,
yet you crawl like little ants
upon the moist earth.

O, great Polka-dot,
We ask of your strength.
We are missing something.
Behold, the magnificent
fruit of hoop-loop!
Fetch it for us,
and you will be praised.

I shall glide across the wind,
and jump over the seas.
I will land in front
of the tall hoop-loop tree

O, the fruit is ripe,
and I shall pluck some
from their branches.

Look! I see great Polka-dot!
O, the grace it possesses,
as it jumps over the seas,
and glides across the wind!

My friends,
I have brought you
the fruit of hoop-loop.
A feast shall be prepared!
Huzzah! Huzzooh!

Set the bowls!
Fill them, fill them!
Paint a picture
of our beloved Polka-dot.
We praise you, we praise you!
Live on with us.

Orange, Purple, and Pink

Orange, purple, and pink
As the great candle of the world is lifted above the horizon
Trees swaying gently in the breeze
The rocking awakens the birds
Moisture never seen up close is floating among our windows
The birch leaf is pulled down slowly
The weight of the drop pulls down, down, down
Pink and orange clouds shift to form fluffy mountains in the distance
Birds peep their early song
Dreams ended peacefully
Streaks of energy stream into every room
Orange, purple, and pink
Turning into blue

Many Mornings I Have Stood Here

Many mornings I have stood here, atop this maple tree.
The cherry blossoms follow behind.
I gaze out upon the sea and feel that something is not right.
Though the mountains encompass this perfect frame.

Many mornings I have stood here, atop this maple tree.
The cherry blossoms follow behind.
Again, and again, each morning I rose,
      only to see the same thing.

Many mornings I have stood here, atop this maple tree.
The cherry blossoms follow behind.
The ocean crashes and the breeze blows.
The tress sway and the leaves swirl.

Many mornings I have stood here, atop this maple tree.
The cherry blossoms follow behind.
You see, in this perfectness, nothing can be changed.
Nothing has for many a moon.

Many mornings I have stood here, atop this maple tree.
The cherry blossoms follow behind.
Though night passes with her twinkling stars,
      and the moon glows on the mountains,
Nothing is different
and nothing will be.

Many mornings I have stood here, atop this maple tree.
The cherry blossoms follow behind.
I must cherish this moment, for winter is coming,
      and departure is sprinting faster.

Many mornings I have stood here, atop this maple tree.
The cherry blossoms follow behind.
I must leave, for I am the sparrow,
      and the sparrow must go.

Many mornings I have stood here, atop this maple tree.
The cherry blossoms follow behind.
Many years back I left, and now I am here.
Hello, ocean!
Hello, mountains!
Hello, hill!
Hello, cherry blossoms!
Hello, maple tree!
Hello, countryside!
May my love for you ring out.
May you stay here and not leave me, as I have left you.

Many mornings I have stood here, atop this maple tree.
The cherry blossoms follow behind.

A Black Rose

In the early morning,
the sun dawns upon the gilded rose garden.
Red,
pink,
yellow,
and white blooms awaken to the dewy rising.

But of all these hues does a black rose catch your eye?
Has there ever been a charcoal bloom etched in your memory?

In a wedding bouquet,
white roses and yarrow are wrapped in a paper of soft green.
The flowers spin round and round.

But of all these hues does a black rose catch your eye?
Has there ever been a charcoal bloom etched in your memory?

On a balcony high above the ground,
overlooking the city,
a red rose is withdrawn and presented to the maiden.
A red rose,
blood red and deeply inviting.
Red,
like blood dripping from a wound.
It delights

But of all these hues does a black rose catch your eye?
Has there ever been a charcoal bloom etched in your memory?

In the country and among the hills,
yellow and pink roses spring to the light,
engulfing children in their sweet,
free scent.
They sway gracefully in the cool,
ocean breeze.

But of all these hues does a black rose catch your eye?
Has there ever been a charcoal bloom etched in your memory?

I doubt it.
Always a place for the light and classic.
When will a new color step forward?

Possibilities

Buildings explode and rubble descends
upon the roads. Fire and flames
add to the chaos, creating a bonfire.

The waves rise high, high, crashing upon the
sand and cliffs. Then higher. Highest.
Falling down and washing everything away.

Plunging down. A simple slip and it's
over. The wind lashes at your cheeks,
bringing tears to your eyes. Only for
a short second. Gone.

I jump as I am brought back. The horrors
took over my body. I am shaking now.
These are the possibilities if we are
not careful. The angers of nature and
war. Of carelessness.

These are the possibilities of life and
death.

Illuminated

I run my fingers along the spines of each shelf.
My fingertip is layered in grime.

I find a dark purple book.
The pages are painted in gold and the gilded lettering shines in the light that seeps in through the window.

I open the treasure and flip a few pages.
An illuminated letter stares back at me.
"H"
The elaborate design in black ink impresses me.
Swirls and curves entwine with each other.

I turn to the next chapter to behold this glory.
"R"
The vines flow freely but twist in an immensely ornate chaos.

I spend my time finding the illumination hidden in the pages.
I cradle the beautiful thought that this glorious sight is in something so permanent as black ink.
Inky,
dark,
black
ink.

Ice Cream

In the hot summer sun by the ocean, atop a hill, a child stands. A chocolate ice cream cone is clutched in their small fingers.

They bring the treat to their mouth. The tongue comes out and licks, scraping off a layer. The cool liquid runs down their throat. It soothes.

The cold chocolate begins to drip down the cone and onto the child's hand. With a quick slurp, it's gone.

Once again the tongue comes out. It digs into the cream, leaving a dent. A soft, cold chunk of the summer delight is mashed between the tongue and the hard pallet. It disappears through the dark tunnel.

The child continues to lick, savoring each moment of a youth's fondest memories.

Icicle

The bitter cold of the arrow sweeps through
the blood of my finger. Paralyzed.

Beautiful clearness reflects and shoots light around
this wonderland.

The ice begins to melt and drips into my hand.
It rolls down my arm and into my jacket.

The slushy mush below my feet has works its way
into my boot.
My toes are frozen.

My fingers run down the jagged arrow.
The cold seeps through so horribly.
With each jagged touch to my finger,
I feel that blood is showing.

The blade suddenly cracks and breaks.
It shatters in front of me.
I shift the fragments with the tops of my feet.

I walk off thinking of that glorious icicle.

Seagull

I turn swiftly in the power, roaring wind.
It ruffles my feathers, cooling my unseen skin.

I dive towards the glistening water.
I break the surface as my claw drags along the glassy sea.

I rise up and swerve.
My wings flap and are raised by the ferocious wind.

I spy some sailboats floating in the water.
I perch on the mast of one.
It rocks left and right.
I sway with it.
The boat takes off.
I squawk and fly away.

The fish below catch my eye.
I swoop down and hold the fish in my beak.
Delicious.

Finally, I come to rest in the water.
I fold my wings and drift with the waves.
I am content.

Goodbye

All things must come to an end. You see, this is the last page of my notebook. I'm not even sure I have enough space to write this poem.

Books come to an end, when you flip the last page and discover it's over. You may not realize, but when you finish a book, you kill it. Shall you open its cover again, it will reawaken.

Fires come to an end. The flames danced brightly, illuminating our faces. But, in the cold morning world, the flickering died down. The embers ceased to glow. All that is left is the ashy sticks that fed it.

Life comes to an end. Yes, indeed. Life. Like it or not there will come a time when things will turn dark. All will be gone, never to be seen again.

So I say goodbye, as I write the final words.

The Zraveler Beep

Thick jungles.
Home to the fwabble vines.
Deepening. Darkening.
A stomach-turning climb to the top.
"But none can stop the Zraveler Beep from reaching the
    mombla sky!"
My voice rings out through the mungle jungle trees.

My travels are nice.
I'm never in a slice.
For I, the Zraveler Beep, am the best at what I do.
I've seen flowers in India,
Quick dances in South America, snow in Alaska,
    and the gentle Bumblers in Greenland.

But, after Mt. Everest, something went wrong,
When I went to the frumpling Mariana Trench.
There were Woobleways and Kabaloopas.
And the graceful Sanafias.
But when I reached the very bottom, I spotted a
    lazdy red submarine.
What they call humans, smackling madly inside.
I don't care to take a picture.
Humans are boring.
But, before I could think, great whoufling metal
    claws snatched after me!
T'was a monster hunter submarine!
I ripped off the claws and threw them to the side.
I escaped as the silly humans chased after their beloved
    snatchers.

After a while,
I longed for my sweet cottage.
Among the fleep ower flowers.
I soon returned to my bed.
My house is draped with my travel trophies.
I possess the thickest photo album in the mubly
      wubly drawer.
I still do travel,
But soon return to "Ye Pabble Cottage."

Ode to Kiwis

I run my fingers down your scratchy brown fur
Cut in two, black seeds
Make a happy circle around a white spot.
Spoon in hand, I scoop one half and bring it to my key to vision.
My eyes narrowed,
I inspect the sour fruit,
Making sure nothing bruised reaches my taste buds.
Am I sure?
I am.
Am I really?
Yes.
No.
Maybe.
A voice inside my head says,
"Stop with the back and forth and get it over with!"
I nod my head in agreement.
My spoon is brought down and shovels through the firm, green fruit,
In almost slow motion, I bring the scoop to my mouth,
Wide, wide open.
The moment approaches.
The moment of delight,
Down go my lips and in goes the fruit.
I bite down.
Flavor explodes,
Filling my mouth.
My mind is flooded with thoughts of this sour, yet amazing experience.
Scoop and eat, scoop and eat,
Soon the skin is nothing but an empty shell.
I reach for the next half of my sour, juicy adventure.

Early Forest Morning

Fire crackling.
The forest pines tower.
A fresh smell fills my lungs.
A quiet moment. Almost a picture. Thinking back.
Forest morning.

Lost in a Dream

Lost. Lost.
Hoops in the air. Chased.
Jump out of zentagle. Run.
I must escape. I can't live here. Lost.
Help me.

Nothing Resists

Nothing resists.
No one resists. Never.
The temptation. Drowning us. Washing over.
To turn the light off for everyone else.
The picture depicts only you.
Nothing resists.

My Freedeom

My freedom.
There at my reach.
A simple pen. Smoothly running across.
Filled with ink, the nib curves gently.
My freedom.

Pushed Around

Pushed around.
People shove. Me, alone.
Not thinking. Pulling, pushing, shoving, thrashed.
You push us around, cruel folk! You invaders.
Never return.

So Credulous

I believed
What they said. Credulous
I believe what they say. Credulous
They laugh. My face red. Humiliation creeps closer
So credulous.

My Bed

The lilies and lily pads tickle my skin.
The cold petals cool my flesh.

My fingers reach down and drag along the murky bottom.
The dirt and dust clog my finger nails.

The sun rays cut into my eyes.
I lurch my head away and blink in the shade.
It washes away the pain.

My head bumps against the banks.
I push away into a patch of algae.
It slips up my feet and my shins and then slides off.
I cringe.

Suddenly,
waves push and shove me across the surface.
I drift into a clump of lilies.
The sweet petals and scent engulf my face.

I realize I am simply drifting in my bed,
nestled in the covers.
I wasn't even asleep.
My greatest imagination always comes in my bed.

A Raindrop Has No Choice

A raindrop doesn't have a very long life
Unlike a bubble
It plummets towards the earth
At an exceedingly fast rate
When a bubble rises up into the air slowly
And takes its time to pop
A raindrop has no choice
When a raindrop hits the ground
It becomes one of many raindrops: a puddle
And that is where it stays
Until it evaporates into the air
And becomes a raindrop again.

California Lilacs

Lilacs sprout.
A rich fragrance about.
A wild call. Echoing around us.
Small yellow beads that bloom on every street.
Soft purple.

www.ingramcontent.com/pod-product-compliance
Lightning Source LLC
Chambersburg PA
CBHW031439040426
42444CB00006B/890